# About the Author

Nikolai N' 'een running his own acc' Naylor Accountancy 2012 after giving up 'don.

'e wanted to run his 'ome point, he just did not 'r when. He wanted to make a 'ice and he did not feel he could do 'is in a big corporate. After being inspired by his friend who had an accounting practice and seeing the difference he made to businesses, he decided to set up his accountancy practice. He had to start by doing everything in his accountancy practice and gradually built up a team as he could afford it, creating the structure required to have a business that operates without him.

As with anything in life, the journey has not been smooth and there will be more bumps in the road to come. He sees these bumps as learnings along the way that strengthens us.

Nikolai has another business, Intelligent Outsourcing, which he started in 2016 and is based in the Philippines which supplies accountancy practices with offshoring accounting teams that work exclusively for them as a partnership that helps accountancy practices grow, enabling them to focus on client relationships and added value work. He has a great team running the business in the Philippines and he is frequently over there. With Nikolai's desire to make a difference not only to the partners/clients and the team, Intelligent Outsourcing also does outreach in the local community with a focus to help educate people out of poverty.

He is married with two teenage kids and a dog and loves spending time with them, especially on holidays when there are no other distractions. He travelled the world for over a year with his wife shortly after getting married, which was a great way to start married life. They did a month's volunteering in Ecuador then travelled around Latin America for 6 months learning Spanish, followed by Fiji, Cook Islands, New Zealand, Australia, Vietnam, Cambodia, Thailand and Malaysia.

Nikolai is a 4th degree black belt in Tae Kwon Do having practiced it since he was a teenager and he goes to classes regularly with his kids. Well-being is especially important to him and he has his daily exercises that he always has to fit in at the start of the day.

Nikolai enjoys learning and did Business Studies at university, then whilst working he studied accounting with the Chartered Institute of Management Accountants and treasury with the Association of Corporate Treasurers. Now he focuses on self-development and consumes loads of different topics and types of material. Being part of a mastermind group helps with the self-development and development of the business.

He has always had a love of traveling, backpacking around Europe and the USA whilst at university. After university, he travelled around the world starting in India, Nepal, and South East Asia with a stop in Australia to work in Sydney for 6 months before resuming traveling around Australia, and New Zealand, finishing with Fiji, Hawaii, LA, and New York.

If you are wondering where "Nikolai" comes from, it is Danish as his mother is from Denmark. The family goes over to Denmark at least once a year to see family there and Nikolai does speak Danish but with an English accent as he mainly grew up in Yorkshire.

# Forward

Hello,

I am excited to introduce you to "Get The Accounting Practice You Want", the first book by Nikolai Naylor - a successful UK accountant, entrepreneur, and valued member of The Accountants' Mastermind community.

Nikolai's book is a treasure trove of insights and practical advice that will help you take your accounting practice to new heights. Drawing on his own experiences as the owner of Naylor Accountancy Services and Intelligent Outsourcing, Nikolai shares the lessons he has learned, the mistakes he has made, and the strategies he has used to create a practice that operates efficiently and effectively, even when he is not directly involved in day-to-day operations.

What sets this book apart is its practicality. Nikolai offers actionable steps that you can use to build a practice that works for you, not the other way around. He shows you how to delegate effectively, build a strong team (Something I am madly passionate about), streamline your processes, and create a practice that is sustainable, scalable, and rewarding.

As the owner of GreenStones and a mentor to many accountants through The Accountants' Mastermind, I can confidently say that this book is a must-read for anyone who wants to build a successful accounting practice. Nikolai's expertise extends far beyond accounting, and his insights will help you take control of your practice and your life.

One of the most inspiring aspects of Nikolai's story is his growth mindset. He is always learning, always striving to improve, and always looking for ways to create more value for his clients and his team. This book is a testament to that mindset, and it is packed with practical advice that will help you achieve your goals and build the practice of your dreams.

"Get The Accounting Practice You Want " is not just a book to read and set aside. It is a call to action. Nikolai's practical advice is designed to help you create a practice that works for you, and the ONLY way to achieve that is to TAKE ACTION on what you learn from these pages.

So, I challenge you to put Nikolai's advice into practice. Use this book as a roadmap to build the practice of your dreams, and don't be afraid to take risks, experiment, and iterate along the way. Building a successful accounting practice takes hard work, dedication, and a willingness to try new things. But with Nikolai's guidance, you can do it.

As someone who has owned an accountancy practice for over two decades and has helped countless accountants through The Accountants' Mastermind, I can tell you that the rewards of building a successful practice are immense. Not just financial rewards but the satisfaction of creating something that provides real value to your clients and your team.

So, read this book, TAKE ACTION, and build the practice you want. I wish you all the best on your journey, and I know that with Nikolai's guidance, you can achieve great things.

Let's Get Started...

Simon Chaplin

Owner at GreenStones Accountants and Founder at The Accountants' Mastermind

# Contents

Introduction ........................................................................ 6

30 ways to ensure you fail at running your accountancy practice effectively! 7

1. YOU ........................................................................ 13

What do you want from your practice? ........................................ 13

Wake up and smell the coffee! ............................................... 15

You cannot make everyone happy! ............................................. 17

Let Go! ...................................................................... 18

Vision ....................................................................... 20

Your Leadership .............................................................. 22

Believe ...................................................................... 27

Trust others ................................................................. 29

Mistakes are inevitable so allow them ........................................ 32

Energy ....................................................................... 35

Perseverance ................................................................. 38

No Procrastination ........................................................... 40

Change course if you must .................................................... 42

Ego .......................................................................... 44

Listen ....................................................................... 46

Self-development .............................................................. 48

Be a great Leader! ........................................................... 51

2. SERVICES ................................................................... 55

3. TEAM ....................................................................... 59

Core Values .................................................................. 64

Letter of expectation ........................................................ 66

Team NOT Employees or staff .................................................. 69

Recruitment and retention .................................................... 70

Create a Leadership team. ........ 72
4. RHYTHM OF THE BUSINESS ........ 75
Daily Huddle ........ 76
Weekly Leadership meetings ........ 77
121 meetings ........ 79
Quarterly Review Meeting ........ 80
Review the Way Forward Plan ........ 82
Key Issues Discussed ........ 84
Annual Way Forward Planning Meeting ........ 86
Rules of a meeting ........ 96
5. BUSINESS STRUCTURE ........ 99
Create systems and procedures ........ 99
Organisational Structure and functions ........ 103
Agendas ........ 106
6. OFFSHORING TEAM and OUTSOURCING ........ 109
Summary ........ 117
Appendix ........ 119
a) Why #hamster? ........ 119
b) Selling your practice? ........ 120
Acknowledgments ........ 121

# Introduction

I have read loads of books, experimented with different ways of operating my accountancy practice Naylor Accountancy Services and we are currently operating it in such a way that I have been able to step right back and focus on strategy and guidance. The day to day is all done by the team which also allows me to focus on my other business, Intelligent Outsourcing.

Nothing in this book is rocket science and it will not rock the world with any amazing new ideas, it is the knowledge I have gained so far in my journey to allow me to create the practice I have now and give me the freedom to focus on what I prefer to spend my time on. It is not perfect and we have not stopped improving how we do things and I am continually learning. The book is here to give you short cuts to reading loads of books and to inspire you that you can make your accounting practice work for you, not you for your accounting practice and if you think you already have it all figured out, there is always room for improvement. This book goes through what we have done in my accountancy practice to get the practice I wanted which is one that does not rely on me. You can use this book like a menu and pick and choose where you prefer to start and gradually add on as you progress. The most important thing for me it is to share **how you can get your accountancy practice 'working for you,' rather than 'you working' for your accountancy practice**.

# 30 ways to ensure you fail at running your accountancy practice effectively!

Before we go through the positive things that you can do to improve your accountancy practice it is important to know the ways you can fail. None of us are perfect and you will no doubt see things in here that you may be doing now or may have done in the past.

How can you make sure you have a bad practice, are stressed, doing all the work, never taking holiday and earning little and ensure you are bored as you are only doing compliance work.

This may seem back to front to you but knowing how you will fail to have the accountancy practice you desire is key to understanding what you must do to get the accountancy practice you deserve if you put the work and effort in.

What 30 things do you need to do to fail?

1. **Never delegate** as you think no one can work as well as you or manage relationships better than you so never allow anyone else to do anything. Take on everything yourself.
2. **Do work for free**. Do it as a favour or because it does not take long to do and you know exactly what to do as you have studied accounting for years and have the necessary expertise. Why should they pay when it is so easy for you to do.
3. **Forget to invoice for work that you agreed a fee on**. You are so busy doing everything you have no time to invoice clients for the actual work you are doing. So, you are getting stressed and working loads of

hours for free. You do not like to invoice as it feels dirty, you like the client and value the friendship so does not feel you should invoice despite having agreed the fee.

4. **Do not chase outstanding payments**. You are so busy you have no time to chase anyone so you just ignore the build of debtors and carry-on doing work for those owing you money. Again, you do not mind doing work for free as you are sure they will realise they need to pay you soon.
5. **Carry on doing work for clients that don't pay** and have no intention to pay you. So, continue to do work for free, be stressed and take time away from paying clients to work with none paying clients.
6. **Put free work or non-paying clients ahead of the clients who are paying on time.** So, you will have less time for paying clients and less time to bring in new paying clients as you are spending your valuable time on non-paying work and clients.
7. **Never increase fees** in line with increased work. You have no time for fee reviews so you are happy to just carry on charging the startup fee when the business was earning less than £50K even though it is now earning £250K per annum now and bookkeeping has increased tenfold.
8. **Allow scope creep** as it is painful for you to do a fee review with clients. You feel uncomfortable, the client may not take it well and they may leave.
9. **Never push yourself out of your comfort zone,** this means you will never move anything forward unless you already feel comfortable with it and know it.

10. You may be **worried about clients leaving** so you do whatever they say even if they are wrong or you end up doing extra work for free.
11. **Keep clients who are unpleasant or cost you money.** These may be people who are not willing to pay for the service they are consuming, are always late with information and always blame you and your team for delays. In other words, no mutual respect.
12. **Do not get rid of poor performing team members**. **Allow bad apples in your team** to continue bringing everyone else down and have no respect for you or the business or clients. Permit them to create negativity in the team.
13. **You have everything in your head** about clients, process, procedures and your plans. You know how everything needs to be done so you do not see the need to set these out in writing once you have trained your team members in it, they have the process in their heads as well.
14. **Everyone uses their own processes with nothing written down**. You do not worry if anyone is off as they will just catch up when they get back and if they should never come back, you are sure someone will be able to work out what they are doing and create their own new process in their head.
15. **Never learn from mistakes or admit them.** You will not admit to your mistakes as you are the boss and your ego will not allow you to be seen as making mistakes.
16. **Your team never learn from their mistakes** and you do not worry about it and do not put in place new processes and procedures or training to ensure it does not happen again.

17. **You do not trust anyone**. You cannot trust your team to do the work so you must micro manage everything.
18. **You have no plan for your accountancy practice** so you have no idea what you want to do in the next 12 months let alone the next 5-10 years.
19. **Procrastinate** about everything so you never make a decision until it is too late.
20. **Only work to the HMRC and Companies House deadline.** You do not care about getting work done and submitted as quickly as possible as you think clients are fine being told their payments to be made the HMRC the day before it is required with no prior warning.
21. **Never listen to clients, ignoring their needs and concerns,** only telling them what you think they want to hear and what you want to tell them. You are only concerned about getting the work done and telling them what to pay HMRC and then move onto then next job.
22. **Never listen to your team** and do not have one to one meetings with your team as you see it as a waste of time.
23. **Do not keep up with changes in accounting regulations** and tax laws.
24. **Do not train your team** or provide them with ongoing professional development opportunities.
25. **Communicate ineffectively** with your team and clients.
26. **Do not invest in technology** to streamline your practice's operations.
27. **Have no idea of your finances** or keep track of your expenses.
28. **Have no vision** for your accountancy practice.
29. **Do not track your performance** or set goals or have KPIs.
30. **Do not invest in your own personal and professional growth.**

I am sure you will see some of the above in you now or in the past. If you don't then are you being honest with yourself? I know I have exhibited most of the above at some point and I have ensured that I work against all of them in a positive way.

# Chapter 1

# YOU

# 1. YOU

## What do you want from your practice?

Do you want an accountancy practice which doesn't rely entirely on you?

That allows you to sleep at night without worrying that Mr Smith had their accounts filed on time.

Do you want a team that can do everything needed in your practice without you even being there? Then you can go on holiday without worrying about anything, recharge your batteries properly and spend quality time with your family.

I know so many accountants who have their own practice who work all the hours possible to keep their clients happy and put their friends and family second. I was one of them. When you first start your practice this is normal as you are the one that has to do everything until you have a sufficient client base to warrant getting more team members to help you. However, most accountants continue to operate like this indefinitely.

For business owners the **main goal is to have a business which is a 'turn key business' that can operate without you being there**. This means that you can focus on what you want to do and that you can easily sell your business. Is this what you want from your accountancy practice?

There are three freedoms that we may be wanting in any combination which are:

1. **Financial** freedom– wanting a certain amount of income in order to enjoy a particular lifestyle that offers.
2. **Time** freedom – wanting more time to focus on things that are important to you and not just spending time on the business. This could be family, a hobby, travel, study, strategy, ... whatever it is for you.
3. **Mind** freedom – wanting peace of mind that all clients are being well looked after and all filings are done on time. All without you needing to get involved.

You may enjoy the technical accounting work so you can always focus on that, get others to focus on the client facing. If you love dealing with client relationships then focus on that and get others in the team to do the work for the clients.

## Wake up and smell the coffee!

Before even looking at creating a "practice that you want" you have to realise that you are the reason that you do not have the practice you want……clear and simple. Do not blame anyone or anything else. Take full responsibility for the fact that you work too many hours, do not see your family, are always thinking of your clients and worried about losing clients and income. If you do not do this then you will never "get the practice you want."

I realised that I was the bottle neck to growing my accountancy practice Naylor Accountancy Services and I had to make changes to my mindset and the structure of the business in order to step away and "get the practice I wanted". This has not been easy to do and I wanted to write this book to give other accountants tips on what I have learnt so far. I say so far because I know we have loads more to do to improve things and I will be learning throughout the journey as we grow Naylor Accountancy Services. This will be through continuous self-development, the leadership team enlightening me and us learning from mistakes that we all inevitably make. You should never be complacent and think you have it all worked out, things are always changing and key is to stay relevant and constantly look to improve.

These quotes are so true and I am sure you can relate to them.

***"Take chances, make mistakes. That's how you grow."***

Mary Tyler Moor

***"The only real mistake is the one from which we learn nothing,"***

Henry Ford

I also like the quote from John Wooden a Hall of Fame basketball player/coach:

"***If You're Not Making Mistakes, then You're Not Doing Anything***."

You will see later in the book that it is key to allow mistakes to be made by others and ensure they learn from them in order to develop and take jobs from you. I know accountants who as soon as someone makes a mistake they say "I knew I should have done it myself, they just don't know how to do it" or ".... they will never learn." This will never allow you to "get the practice you want."

See sections "Let Go!" and "Team."

Realisation of what you want and what you need to do is critical. If you are happy where you are with your practice you do not need to change anything then do not read any further. You probably should carry on reading but if you do not think you need to change anything or you are blaming circumstances that you think are out of your control, then you are never going to "get the practice you want". You must "wake up and smell the coffee" and realise you are in control; you are accountable and you are able to change things!

Normally the pain you experience has to be big enough for you to make a change. Unless of course you are very forward looking, have a vision for you personally and your accounting practice that pushes you to make the changes with a plan. If you continue to read this book then you will more than likely be in this category of forward-thinking accountants.

**You cannot make everyone happy!**

You have to realise that you cannot make everyone happy. You must do what is right and consider others but that does not mean that you have to do what they want you to do. You must never be scared of making people unhappy as people do not like change and they have their own opinion. You should listen to what other people have to say and take it into consideration but you must make up your "own" mind on what you want to do and then go for it.

Some team members and clients will not be happy with change but speak with them and potentially loose them to move forward.

or later maybe 04 as its about above BUT MIGHT PUT PEOPLE OFF READING?

does this need to be here?

Story of a team member against change

I had a team member of Naylor Accountancy Services who was totally against having an offshoring team. She was always negative saying "they will not know where to allocate a Boots receipt when they do the bookkeeping." My answer was always straight forward, they will use Google and learn.

They also hated our daily huddles when we started them and they had a face like thunder throughout all the meetings making it clear of their displeasure to all including our Philippines team.

That team member did not last long after introducing the offshore accounting team and I would not have compromised our development for that team member. We would not have the business we have today if we had not created our offshore accounting team with what became Intelligent Outsourcing.

**Let Go!**

Letting go is the most difficult for accountants especially as we like to be in control and we think that we are the best at it. We do not want to trust someone else to do the project or to make sure things are done on time, we want to do it.

We think we are the only person who can deal with clients or a specific client. In some cases, this may be true but first let go and then if you still want to keep a client that is kicking off go back to meeting with them but get all the work done by the team. Your team will only learn to do the work you are doing once you allow them to do it and train them in it, so proactively ensure you delegate and train the team members in what you do and let go so they become responsible for carrying out the job.

Story of not letting go.

I did all the Ltd company annual filings, Ltd company set ups, changes at Companies House for address, directors, shares, etc. I carried on doing this even though I had hired someone fulltime to do bookkeeping and some other administrative work. Then a year in when I was really swamped with work, I gave the person a small Company Secretariat job to do. She did it well and asked me why I had not given her that type of work sooner? I realised then that I had thought I was the only one that could possibly do the work as no one else would be able to figure it out....... **how wrong was I**.... why did I even think like that? So, I gave her all the Company Secretariat and she did it for years before we handed it over to our administrative team in our Intelligent Outsourcing offshore team for Naylor Accountancy Services. They do a great job and can figure out anything using the Company Secretariat system we have. I "let go" and put "trust" in the people that I "delegated" the work and they became "accountable" for the work willingly giving them empowerment.

## Vision

As the business owner you must know what you want from your accountancy practice. Look at what you enjoy doing, what income you need to take out of the business, how much time do you want to spend with family and friends, what holidays would you like to go on.

As the business owner you must be clear about what you want before you can guide others towards a vision of the future that they will be part of. Once you have a Leadership Team, you must have them create the Vision statement with you in an Annual Way Forward meeting. This is key to get their buy in and get them to highlight issues and other things you may not have thought of.

What do you want the business to look like in 10 years' time? This is the first thing to focus on as once you have this then you know what it should look like in 3 years' time and then the 1-year plan is easier to create. It is amazing what you can achieve if you look out 10 years... You can really think big if that is what you and your leadership team want. You may be more interested in maintaining what you have with you not working more than a certain number of hours and having an A team to run the accountancy practice. However, if you open it up to the Leadership team to help create the Vision you will be surprised what they may come up with especially if they are bought into the practice and want to further increase their personal wealth.

I have been told by others have a 5-year vision and then go back from there. However, to me this is too limiting as you cannot achieve as much in 5 years as you can in 10 years. If you only focus on 5 years you will not know what the ultimate destination is. With 10 years you really can play around and work out what you and your leadership team would like as a business. Why 10 years is good is you can then plan back what you need to do to get there, think about your journey, opportunities will pop up and ideas for you to get there which may never have appeared if you were limited to 5 years.

Having said all this, if you are only interested in looking 5 years forward then do that. You may be coming up to retirement and may not be interested in growth. I love looking to the future and always have planned to build a legacy business that will outlast me, so I want to look as far ahead as possible.

This is a basic way to create your Vision is set out below, you want it to become something that you can see, feel and experience as if you are already there. So, the more detail the better, after all it is a Vision like creating a picture of what you want it to look like in the future.

***"A vision is a compass that guides you through the journey of building a successful business."*** - Simon Sinek.

## Your Leadership

Leadership is all about influence and you must have followers. Without you getting you're a team onboard with the vision and them having the motivation to move towards the vision through executing the plan, then you will never get there.

You cannot create anything of value with just one person, you need a team for that. That is why leadership is all about influence.

John Maxwell who is probably the world's biggest expert on leadership says, ***"everything rises and falls on leadership."***

As a leader always look at how you can add value to your team members. This could be giving them advice, connecting them with others, giving them a project to develop them, giving them more responsibility, let them know when they make mistakes and ask what they learn from it and what would they do differently next time.

Look to create leaders within your accountancy practice as this will allow you to ensure someone is taking responsibility for certain areas and you can take something off your projects as they will take it on and develop it. To be a truly great leader you must create and develop leaders, not just have minions. If you are always the hero this will just mean the business can only sustain itself with you being there as you will be the know it all in the business. This can crush others as you will then probably not allow anyone to air their views as you just tell them how it must be done, no ifs or buts.

You must be a "multiplier" not a "diminisher" as a leader.

The terms "leadership multiplier" and "leadership diminisher" were coined by Liz Wiseman in her book "Multipliers: How the Best Leaders Make Everyone

Smarter". These terms refer to two distinct types of leaders and their impact on their teams.

A **leadership multiplier** is a leader who amplifies the intelligence and capabilities of their team. They create a culture of trust and empowerment, encourage team members to take ownership of their work, and provide opportunities for learning and growth. They seek to bring out the best in their team members and help them reach their full potential.

In contrast, a **leadership diminisher** is a leader who restricts the intelligence and capabilities of their team. They tend to micromanage, hoard information, and create a culture of fear and dependency. They often think they know best and don't trust their team members to make decisions. As a result, team members may feel disempowered, undervalued, and unmotivated.

<u>Story of a diminisher</u>

I did an acquisition of an accountancy practice and the owner of it was a diminisher. They did not believe anyone could do the accounts properly, could do the invoicing or could file accounts, they had to do it all. The practice was in a real mess when we took it on and all the accounts were being done up to 12 months after the yearend every month...... they had changed the yearend dates by a month at Companies House which allowed an extra 3 months on top of the normal 9 month filing deadline. I did not even know you could do this...... They had not invoiced loads of clients for work they carried out in the previous years so they were getting stressed doing work for clients for zero money!!!! Had they allowed other accountants that worked for them to invoice once they completed the work, do peer reviews and allow them to do some of the accounts they did as well as submit to HMRC and Companies House then they would probably not have needed to sell. They were selling as they could not cope with running the practice. They did not empower anyone and they were constantly blaming others for anything that went wrong.

The evidence suggests that leadership multipliers are generally more effective than leadership diminishers. This is because they create an environment in which everyone can contribute to their full potential, which leads to better results, increased engagement, and higher levels of creativity and innovation. By contrast, leadership diminishers may limit the potential of their teams, leading to lower morale, less productivity, and missed opportunities.

Here are some examples of leaders who are considered to be leadership multipliers:

1. Satya Nadella, CEO of Microsoft - Nadella is known for his ability to empower his team members and encourage them to take risks and innovate. He has created a culture of collaboration and openness, which has led to Microsoft's recent successes.

2. Mary Barra, CEO of General Motors - Barra is known for her focus on empowering her team members and creating a culture of trust and

transparency. She has worked to break down silos within the organization and encourage cross-functional collaboration.

3. Reed Hastings, CEO of Netflix - Hastings is known for his ability to attract and retain top talent, as well as his focus on innovation and experimentation. He encourages his team members to take ownership of their work and provides opportunities for learning and growth.

In contrast, here are some examples of leaders who are considered to be leadership diminishers:

**1.** Steve Jobs, co-founder of Apple - Jobs was known for his micromanagement and his tendency to hoard information. He was a brilliant innovator, but his leadership style could be limiting to his team members. Watch the movie Steve Jobs if you do not believe this.

2. Jeff Immelt, former CEO of General Electric - Immelt was criticized for his tendency to centralize decision-making and his focus on short-term results. He was seen as a leader who limited the potential of his team members.

3. Travis Kalanick, former CEO of Uber - Kalanick was known for his aggressive leadership style and his tendency to create a culture of fear and aggression. He was criticized for his treatment of team members and for limiting the potential of his team members.

As the leader of your accountancy practice, you must think who you want to develop internally into a leader and if you need to bring in someone to a leadership position what are you looking for. You may want someone you can develop and mold or someone that can come straight in with little guidance.

If you are a small practice you may not be in a position to develop a leadership team but you must think of your leadership style and your impact on others.

"***Leadership is the capacity to translate vision into reality.***"

Warren Bennis

## Believe

You must **believe in yourself, the vision and others**. This is absolutely critical! If you do not believe in yourself then you have no hope in getting others on board with your plans.

This means you must believe that you are capable of achieving what you are setting out to accomplish with a plan and team in place to do this. You must believe you have the skillset needed and if you are missing any knowledge, you must believe you can learn it. Of course, you must then learn whatever you are lacking knowledge in, that will be part of your personal plan.

Once you believe in yourself, your capabilities and knowledge then you need to ensure you **believe in the Vision** for the business you create yourself or ideally with your leadership team is achievable in the timescales you have set out with a plan in place. You must believe 100% in your vision or you will not bring others along with it and focus on it. If you do not believe in the vision, you will make excuses why you are no longer going to make it rather than create solutions to get you there.

Finally, you must have a **team around you that you believe in,** are able to get you to where you want to go or at least for now. You will more than likely need to bring more team members in and change team members roles as you grow and progress towards your 10-year vision. Key is to have a team in place that you believe will be able to learn and develop to help you move along your plan for the business. The team members will then feel that you believe in them and they will step up. If they don't then you will need to have a conversation with them and that is a different issue (see letter of expectation).

***"Believe you can and you're halfway there."***

Theodore Roosevelt

## Trust others

This is key to growing the practice you want and being able to let go and delegate projects and responsibilities. First you need to "believe" they can do what is required and then you need to "trust" them to do whatever it is you need them to do and give them autonomy where required.

The team may not do projects perfectly to start with as they have to learn and they may not be as efficient as you are and you may lose touch of the coal face (what is happening with every client), but you must trust others as this makes them grow and develop!!! They will take on the responsibility you give them if they have your businesses core values and are capable (see A-Team players). If they don't have your core values and are not capable then should you have them in your team at all? Trusting others is similar to believe in others, difference is you cannot trust someone in your team if you do not believe they are capable of doing the project etc.

You can believe in someone but still not trust them to do something and this is your issue! You must trust in order to "let go." Trust can be misplaced. If it is, then re-assess and take the action required.

Story of not trusting your team

I purchased a practice in 2021 and the owner did not trust any of her team to complete projects or do file accounts or to invoice. She said she was the only one "capable" od doing all of that. The practice was a mess! She was a massive bottle neck and to boot they did not operate any systems (see Systems). All accounts were done up to the extended 12 months deadline created by them changing the yearend date at Companies House by a day which gave them another 3 months to file – I did not even know you could do this.... Clients were chasing for their accounts as they were concerned, they would get penalties and they did not know what tax to pay. HMRC were constantly sending letters of tax payment reminders for clients as they were only told about the tax that had to be paid on the day it needed paying or if they were lucky a couple of days prior.... We had never received so many letters from HMRC before. To top it all we found out that the acquired practice had not invoiced loads of clients for work they did 1 or 2 years earlier. So, they were having all the stress of working to a deadline for no reward at all! They were acting like a charity.

I was flabbergasted when it all sunk in as I could not understand how they survived or put bread on the table as they still had to pay team members salaries, pay bills and live.

Had the practice owner trusted her team to file accounts without her final review, she sat on a review for months until the deadline if they managed to do the work early, then the client would have known their tax payment due in good time and there would be no stress.

If she had trusted the team members to invoice the client as soon as they completed the work, they would not have done work for free!

If they trusted and believed in the team they would not have been stressed as owners and have to do everything last minute which is really bad for your wellbeing as well as service to the client.

If you trust others then others are more likely to trust you. We all have accounting practices and our clients must trust us in order for them to give us the data and information they do. So, the quicker someone trusts you the more likely you will take them on as a client.

If you cannot trust your team to do jobs, then how can clients trust you and the team? Trust goes many ways and before people trust you, you must trust them.

***"People do business with people they know, like and TRUST."***

Dale Carnegie.

## Mistakes are inevitable so allow them

You and your team will make mistakes and you cannot stop that however hard you try. In fact, most businesspeople will say without making mistakes they would not be where they are now. Reason for this is that they learn from mistakes and makes sure as much as is possible that they never happen again.

So do not beat yourself up or get mad at team members for making them, allow them to make mistakes.

Key to your team members making mistakes is they must learn from them and not make the same mistake again. This is the same for you.

As Henry Ford famously said, "**The only real mistake is the one from which we learn nothing**."

When you and your team mistakes then everyone must own up to them straight away and not hide them. You want everyone to be open and if they know you are not going to discipline them for making a mistake and view mistakes as inevitable but that you want all to learn from them, then they will be open. I have one caveat with my team and that is that as long as they have not violated any of our core values, we will always support them with anything they have done.

We have what we call "project perfect" which is where we record all mistakes made when they are made. This enables us to see what has gone wrong centrally. Then in our weekly meeting we discuss the issue that created the mistake and once we have got to the bottom of it then we look to see what solution we can implement to ensure that it does not happen again. This could mean adding an extra step to one of our processes, ensuring everyone gets training in a certain element, etc.

You do not want team members to go below the line (see OARBED) and deny the mistake or blame others for it. You want everyone including yourself to take ownership of mistakes and issues and only by doing this will you or they ensure that they improve and take action to ensure it does not happen again.

**"More people would learn from their mistakes if they weren't so busy denying them."**

**Tom Ziglar**

Story of not admitting mistakes

The practice owner of the accountancy practice owner would never admit any mistake and only blamed others for it. I realised this straight away as we are always using OARBED (see OARBED) with the team and I will call people out if they are not taking responsibility and blaming others or denying whatever. This blame was for virtually everything, from why the practice was in such a mess to why clients were leaving. The worst was she was blaming the team as well as clients……. she was the business owner so everything comes back to them. As the business owner any mistake or issue is ultimately your responsibility so you want to learn from mistakes and develop you, team and the business. I also knew that she would be blaming me for things to others……. she was Teflon……perfect so she could make no mistake, only others could. This was also the big issue with "trust" as highlighted in the above story on trust.

I learned a lot of painful lessons from the acquisition. I worked long hours and the team worked constantly to improve everything and we turned it all around in less than a year. I would never want to go through the pain of that acquisition again! But I would not change what happened as I and the rest of the team learned so much and it made us realise how good and robust our processes and systems were. We have improved them since then.

I mention this because one reason I am writing this book is so that you can learn from my mistakes as well as what I have found to work for me on my journey.

**"Smart people learn from their mistakes. But the real sharp ones learn from the mistakes of others."**

Brandon Mull.

**Energy**

As the owner of the practice, you must have energy to ensure you are able to run your business. You also want the energy to spill over to others so they see urgency in matters that require it.

Key is your wellbeing. So, ensure you get enough sleep, keep fit and eat healthily. I am not going to go into any details here as I am not a personal trainer or wellbeing guru but I will give some tips and examples that work for me.

Exercise is any movement of your body, from a regular gentle walk to boxercise, whatever you do it is good, just do something.

Stretching is really good for you and worth doing regularly. Stretching and some exercise helps you those back and neck pains you get from sitting too much in front of a computer. Do not sit for hours as you must move your body......standing desk, answering calls standing up, stand up meetings, get up to get drinks, walk to talk to people in your office instead of messaging them, this all helps.

Key is not to just sit all day, for example if you are sitting all day at work at your desk, you drive to work sitting in your car, come home and sit to eat dinner followed by sitting to watch TV at night. We all do a lot of sitting. Look to fit in at least 30 minutes a day to do some form of exercise which does not involve sitting.

When you need energy bursts do a "starfish." This is lying on the ground with your legs apart and arms apart like a starfish and rest, closing your eyes. Only do this for up to 20 minutes, so like a nap but lying down. It is like recharging your batteries. Once you get up you feel like you have so much more energy. I do this when I come back from work and I am shattered especially if I will be going to my Tae Kwon-do class that evening

Before doing an online seminar or online meeting that you need to have energy for jump up and down to get your blood pumping it gives you more life and you will come across livelier. - Breath exercise sigh

If you need all the attendees of a meeting to forget whatever else they have on their mind and focus on the meeting then get them all to do three deep breaths at start of a meeting. I have done this one a few occasions in our leadership weekly meetings, be aware your Ds in the DiSC profile will not like this so much (see Chapter in Team on Profiling).

Sleeping is so critical to your health, productivity and general wellbeing. You can still perform relatively well if you have not eaten for 24 hours but if you have not slept for 24 hours then that has a massive impact on you. Again, I am no expert on this but here are a few tips I have learned:

- Never turn the light on once you have gone to bed. So, when you go to the toilet refrain from turning the light on as it will wake you up from your groggy state and it takes ages for you to get back to sleep. I learnt this whilst at university as I was really bad at sleeping at night. It has meant that I walk around in the dark and have to feel my way around, if it is a hotel that I am not used to the lay out this can be interesting when locating the toilet.......I have whacked my shins and walked into doors..... I will never stand up to pee as I am sure my accuracy is no good in the dark, so top tip for males is sit down when you pee at night so you do not need to turn the light on. Sorry if that is too much to share, but it is top tip.

- Blue light is bad. Do not look at your devices before bed and certainly turn them off.
- Have a dark and cold room. It is best to have the window on a latch to let some fresh air in.
- Do not drink coffee or have caffeine at least 6 hours before you go to bed and a lot say do not have after 12pm. It all depends on your tolerance to caffeine.
- Avoid large meals, nicotine, and alcohol before bedtime. These substances can disrupt your sleep and prevent you from feeling fully rested.
- Do not eat sugary things before bed, nuts or other slow-release foods are best if you must eat something.

"***Energy and persistence conquer all things.***"

Benjamin Franklin

**Perseverance**

Be stubborn keep going as long as you keep improving as a person and you still "believe" in what you are doing and retain the "vision". Life and business are a roller coaster and you have to take the downs as well as the ups. If you are not happy doing this you should not have your own accountancy practice. You will have times whey you may think "why am I doing this," I know I have; the importance is you keep focussed.

Perseverance is important in any business because it allows you to stay focused on your goals, overcome obstacles, and persist through challenging times. To be successful with your accountancy practice you must understand that setbacks and failures are inevitable, but with perseverance, you can learn from these experiences and move forward towards achieving your vision.

Several famous business writers advocate the importance of perseverance in business, including:

- Stephen Covey - the author of the best-selling book "The 7 Habits of Highly Effective People," which emphasizes the importance of persistence and determination in achieving success.
- Napoleon Hill - best known for his book "Think and Grow Rich," which is based on the idea that success is achieved through persistence and the refusal to give up in the face of adversity.
- Seth Godin - a prolific writer and speaker on topics related to marketing and entrepreneurship. He often emphasizes the importance of perseverance and resilience in the face of failure.

*"Many of life's failures are people who did not realize how close they were to success when they gave up."*

Thomas A. Edison

"Whatever desision I make is the right one for now" ->

Mark

**No Procrastination**

Procrastination can be a major obstacle to success in any business, as it can lead to missed opportunities, missed deadlines, and a general lack of productivity. In order to achieve success for your accountancy practice, it is important to avoid procrastination and to stay focused on your goals and tasks.

It is important to realise that some personalities which you can get from a DiSC profile (see chapter on Team) will take longer to come to decisions as they will want to analyse, talk through, have time to think about things, read, do research, etc. before they will naturally come to a decision. As the business owner it is your responsibility to push these people forward, allowing them some time to deliberate but not so much time as it becomes an issue.

I have this in my Intelligent Outsourcing leadership team and it can be frustrating as I can see a clear way forward but I need to bring them with me. I have had to drag some people through on occasions and they have not liked that which meant they were not 100% bought into the decision but on one occasion it was costing us £500 per month so I could not allow it to continue. If I had allowed the team member to procrastinated further it would have cost the business more money and no decision would have been made.

It is key to make a decision and not be in limbo doing nothing. The decision may not be the right one but if it is not, you either make it the right one or change the decision. It is worse not to do anything, important thing is to decide and move forward.

Some of the most famous business writers advocate the importance of avoiding procrastination include some of my favourite authors such as:

- Brian Tracy - a motivational speaker and author who has written extensively on the topic of productivity and time management. His book "Eat That Frog!" emphasizes the importance of tackling the most difficult tasks first and avoiding procrastination.
- Stephen Covey - as mentioned earlier, is the author of "The 7 Habits of Highly Effective People." One of the habits he emphasizes is "begin with the end in mind," which encourages individuals to focus on their goals and take action quickly in order to achieve them.
- Tony Robbins - a well-known motivational speaker and author who often emphasizes the importance of taking immediate action in order to achieve success. He argues that procrastination is a major obstacle to success and that taking action quickly is essential for achieving one's goals.

***"You may delay, but time will not."***

Benjamin Franklin

Action is the only answer

Bez Amazon?

**Change course if you must**

Business and life are a journey towards a vision and things change so you may need to change your plans as suddenly you realise your sat navigation is taking you down a dirt track to nowhere or worse directing you off a cliff....... Some people will carry on the dirt track until they realise, they are totally lost and others will keep going further and further off track as it was the plan and they must follow it.  Yes, you must create a plan and follow it but you must be aware if you are on the wrong track and make necessary changes.

In the context of business and your accountancy practice, it is important to have a plan, but it is equally important to be willing to adjust that plan as circumstances change. Here are some things that could make a business plan need to be changed:

- Market conditions: If the market changes, for example, if a new competitor enters the market, or there is a change in consumer demand, the business plan may need to be adjusted to reflect these new conditions.
- Financial considerations: If the business is not meeting its financial targets, the plan may need to be revised to address the issues that are preventing the business from achieving its goals.
- Internal factors: Changes in personnel, processes, or technology can all impact the business plan, and may require adjustments to ensure that the plan remains relevant and achievable.
- External factors: Political, economic, or social changes can also impact a business plan. For example, changes in regulations or trade policies can impact a business's ability to operate in certain markets and may

require adjustments to the plan. This can be seen recently with Covid lock downs.

I have had to ensure we change our business plans in Naylor Accountancy Services and Intelligent Outsourcing when I could see there was a major issue. Some in the leadership were not happy as we set out the plan at the start of the year in the Annual Way Forward meeting. Be aware of people's profiles as you will know the team members who will struggle to change plans. Again, this highlights the need to profile your team, see chapter on Team, as it helps understand how to . interact with them to bring them along.

In summary, it's important to have a plan, but it's equally important to be willing to adjust that plan as circumstances change. By staying flexible and adapting to new conditions, you can stay competitive and achieve your goals over the long term.

***"Failed plans should not be interpreted as a failed vision. Visions don't change, they are only refined. Plans rarely stay the same and are scrapped or adjusted as needed. Be stubborn about the vision, but flexible with your plan."***

John C. Maxwell

## Ego

Keeping your ego in check is essential as an accountancy practice owner because it allows you to make rational decisions and prioritize the success of the business over personal pride or ego. If you let your ego, get in the way, it can lead to a variety of negative outcomes, including:

- Poor decision-making: When you let your ego take over, you may make decisions that are not in the best interest of the business but rather based on personal preferences or desires.
- Lack of teamwork: If you have a big ego, it can make it difficult to work with others effectively. You may be more concerned with getting your own way than working collaboratively with your team to achieve the best outcomes.
- Inability to learn and grow: Having a big ego can make it difficult to take feedback or criticism, which can hinder your ability to learn and grow as a business owner.
- Damage to relationships: If you let your ego get in the way of your interactions with team members, partners, or customers, it can damage relationships and ultimately harm your business.

In contrast, when you keep your ego in check, you are better able to make decisions that prioritise the success of your accountancy practice, work effectively with others in your team, learn and grow, and maintain positive relationships. It allows you to stay humble, open-minded, and receptive to feedback, all of which are valuable traits in the business world.

***"Check your ego at the door. The ego can be the great success inhibitor. It can kill opportunities, and it can kill success."***

Dwayne Johnson (The Rock)

## Listen

Listening is an essential trait to have in any business, especially as an accountancy practice owner, because it helps you build strong relationships with your team, clients/customers, and partners. It enables you to make informed decisions based on feedback and insights. Here are three reasons why listening is important in any business:

1. **Builds trust and rapport**: When you listen to others, it shows that you value their opinions and perspectives. This can help build trust and rapport, which is crucial for fostering strong relationships in business and especially an accountancy practice as clients see you as an expert and someone they must trust.
2. **Provides valuable insights**: Listening to feedback from team members, clients/customers, and partners can provide valuable insights into what is working well and what needs improvement. This information can help you make informed decisions and improve the overall success of the business.
3. **Promotes innovation**: Listening to diverse perspectives and ideas can promote innovation by providing fresh ideas and approaches to problem-solving. This has been so useful for me.

Be aware that most people when in conversation will be thinking of what they want to say in replying to what the person is saying instead of really listening to the person and asking further to get more information or just to hear the full story. You miss out if you only look to reply with our own story and some people call this "topper" i.e., my story is better than yours.... I used to always do this and I had to consciously stop myself. I now write down what I want to bring up if I think it is important in a business setting otherwise, I will forget as

I will be asking further questions and letting the person let me tell me everything before I go back to what I may want to say. If you are a “topper” then be aware that you are and try to keep yourself in check.

This quote by Stephen R. Covey highlights this:

***"Most people do not listen with the intent to understand; they listen with the intent to reply."***

Stephen R. Covey

Listening is important as a means of effective communication and influence, understanding, and building relationships. As the accountancy practice owner, listening can help you create a positive and productive work environment, make informed decisions, and ultimately drive the success of the business.

***"The art of conversation lies in listening."***

Malcolm Forbes

## Self-development

As a leader, continuous self-development is crucial for several reasons. First and foremost, it helps you stay relevant and adapt to the ever-changing business landscape. It also helps you stay engaged and motivated, sets a good example for your team, and allows you to improve your skills and knowledge, which leads to better decision-making and performance. It also helps you create the accountancy practice vision.

Here are five reasons why continuous self-development is important for you as a leader:

1. **Keeps You Relevant**: As a leader, it's important to keep up with the latest trends and best practices in your industry. Continuous self-development helps you stay relevant and ensures that you are able to lead your team effectively.
2. **Increases Your Knowledge and Expertise**: Self-development helps you gain new knowledge and skills that can help you become a better leader. By continuously learning and improving, you can enhance your expertise and provide better guidance to your team.
3. **Boosts Your Confidence**: When you continuously self-develop, you gain a sense of confidence and self-assurance. This confidence can help you make better decisions and inspire your team to follow your lead.
4. **Helps You Build a Stronger Team**: As you develop your leadership skills, you'll be better equipped to build a strong and cohesive team. You'll be able to identify your team members' strengths and weaknesses and provide the support they need to succeed.
5. **Encourages Innovation and Creativity**: Self-development can help you become more innovative and creative in your leadership approach. By

exploring new ideas and ways of doing things, you can inspire your team to think outside the box and come up with new and innovative solutions to problems.

Self-development helps you as a leader to develop the skills and mindset needed to adapt to change and overcome challenges. Always pursue self-development however you digest it, reading, listening, watching or attending. There are loads out there now that is free with podcasts and YouTube and others like books, Kindle, audio, Blinkist and of course good old face to face in the form of workshops, seminars, conferences and mastermind groups.

I am always listening to audio books, podcasts and YouTube programs about business, leadership, management and more. Your smartphone is amazing and you can harness it to help you self-develop and listen to educational items whilst you are doing daily chores, walking the dog, exercising, driving, doing gardening or whatever. Invest in some good headphones that you can easily carry around with you and you can learn anywhere!

I find Blinkist, Audible, Kindle, YouTube and podcasts so useful for my self-development as well as accounting conferences and my mastermind group. The amazing thing with YouTube is you can actually listen and of course see the old greats in persona like Napoleon Hill, Jim Rohn, Earl Nightingale, Stephen Covey and others that have passed away. Plus, you have those still with us like Brian Tracey, John Maxwell, Simon Sinek, Shawn Acher, Tony Robbins, Robert Greene and everyone else. The amazing thing is, you can hear exactly what they say, how they say it and feel a closer connection to their message which you can only better if you were in the room with them. I subscribe to YouTube so I do not need to listen to adverts and I tend to always listen on my phone rather than watch them, so I can do other things at the same time that do not require too much focus like driving, chores around the house and gardening

***"Leadership and learning are indispensable to each other."***

John F. Kennedy

## Be a great Leader!

Being a great leader is something I am always aspiring to be and if we are in a leadership position, we should always be thinking how we can be better.

To be a great leader you must possess or develop a combination of skills and traits that inspire and guide your team towards success. A great leader is someone who not only has a clear vision but also effectively communicates and motivates others to achieve their goals. Here are some essential qualities and tips on how to be a great leader some of which we have touched on in more detail already and this brings them all together:

1. **Vision**: A great leader has a clear vision for the future and inspires others to work towards that vision.
2. **Communication**: Good communication skills are essential for any leader. The ability to articulate ideas and goals clearly, listen actively, and provide feedback effectively are key to building strong relationships with team members. See the chapter on "Rhythm of the Business" as this creates the environment and tools to aid communication.
3. **Empathy**: A great leader understands the needs and feelings of others and is able to empathise with them. This allows the leader to create a positive work environment where team members feel valued and motivated.
4. **Adaptability**: The ability to adapt to changing circumstances is critical for a leader. Great leaders are able to pivot quickly and make decisions in a dynamic and fast-paced environment.

5. **Accountability**: A great leader takes responsibility for their actions and decisions and is willing to admit when they are wrong. This builds trust and respect among team members.
6. **Courage**: Leaders must have the courage to take risks and make difficult decisions, even when faced with uncertainty or opposition.
7. **Continuous Learning**: A great leader is always seeking to learn and improve, both personally and professionally. This allows the leader to stay ahead of the curve and lead with confidence.

***"The greatest leader is not necessarily the one who does the greatest things. He is the one that gets the people to do the greatest things."***

Ronald Reagan

# Chapter 2

# SERVICES

## 2. SERVICES

I am only going to mention accounting services and my thoughts about them on a very basic level on what has worked for us so far.

**Key compliance just done** – you should not worry about this and just know your team will be doing all the compliance required to service the clients in the quickest speed possible. Excellent service is required and this will allow you to do so much more with clients if you want to, the added value work. In Naylor Accountancy Services we have our offshore team with Intelligent Outsourcing do all our compliance work with our UK team focussed on the client relationship and added value work. See chapter on Offshore Team.

**Bookkeeping** – I would always recommend accountancy practices do bookkeeping service for their clients and the reason for this is that if done properly it ensures the yearend accounts and management accounts are easily done as you do not need to correct anything or chase bookkeeping to be done. Make sure you use technology to make this easy with the likes of Dext for client to get copies of invoices into online accounting systems. This is also another fee making service that you can easily add on by creating an offshore team.

Again, in Naylor Accountancy Services we have our offshore team with Intelligent Outsourcing do all our bookkeeping work and they connect directly with the clients to get information that is missing. See chapter on Offshore Team.

**Added value services –** these are key to keeping your clients engaged, growing, tax efficient and ensuring that your accountancy practice is relevant in this tech age. This includes management reporting, budgets, cashflow forecasts, board meetings, business planning, organisational review, succession planning and more.

# Chapter 3

# TEAM

# 3. TEAM

## Build an A-Team

I loved the "A Team" TV series as a kid and the music is always in my head when I see "A-Team" and I have a vision of an angry BA saying, "you fool Murdock!."

Just thinking of the 80's TV series the A Team, everyone had their own role in that team and special skills and together they were the A Team who could do anything, build anything and get the job done. Hannibal was the leader and ensured everyone was doing the right thing to make their adventure a success. You are Hannibal, the cigar chewing leader and you have your specialist team around you who must do what they are good at and are assigned to do to ensure the job is done.

Have you got your "A-Team" around you? Are they doing what they are best at?

Make sure you know what you want your A-Team to do and how many people you need.

Create an **Avatar** for each team member you would want in your A-Team. You should definitely do this if you are wanting to hire a new person or promote from within, but you can also do this if you already have a team to ensure all are in the correct role.

The avatar is a list of everything you want the person in a particular role to do and your ideal profile of that person. Remember you will never find the perfect fit; you want someone who can grow and develop and move forward with your business. Key is having someone in your A-Team who has great attitude, with the capability and understanding of what is required of them in the role and who know their weak areas of knowledge and understanding which they must develop. Development will be through your or others mentoring and self-learning. You really do want proactive team members who are capable of self-learning. Mindset of a person in your A-Team is key as you cannot train this. They must of course fit your core values which we will talk about later.

Write a **letter of expectations** of what you will be expecting of the person in the role. This is everything that you want to see from them.

For example - attitude to other team members (e.g. respectful); how they dress (e.g. casual smart; shirt and tie); personal hygiene (e.g. not smell of BO); clean clothes; punctual; speak to clients once a month; meet clients at least once a year in an annual accounts review meeting; not be drunk at work or be high; work in the office at least 3 days per week; be active in team meetings; answer emails within 24 hours; if sick let the team know by 9.30am; book holidays at least 7 days in advance; always ensure someone can cover your work if you are on holiday; answer phone calls within 4 rings; study ACCA; carry out at least 4 hours of self-learning per month; if you have an issue bring it up withing 24 hours; if you need to discipline a subordinate do so within 24 hours;

It is worth **profiling your team** as this helps ensure your A-Team works most effectively together. It allows you all to gain a deep understanding of the skills, strengths, weaknesses, and personalities of each team member. Profiling can be done through various means, such as assessments, surveys, and feedback sessions. Here are some reasons and benefits to profiling your team:

1. **Improved Communication**: Profiling can help team members understand each other's communication styles and preferences. This knowledge can reduce misunderstandings and conflicts, leading to improved communication.

2. **Enhanced Team Performance**: Profiling can help team members recognize their strengths and weaknesses, allowing them to work on improving their skills. This can lead to enhanced team performance as each member can contribute their best.

3. **Better Team Dynamics**: Profiling can help identify any conflicts or tensions between team members. This knowledge can be used to address these issues and foster better team dynamics.

4. **Effective Project Assignment**: Profiling can help team leaders understand each member's skills and strengths, enabling them to assign projects that suit each individual's abilities. This can increase project efficiency and productivity.

5. **Personal Development**: Profiling can provide team members with valuable feedback about their skills and personality traits. This knowledge can help individuals work on their personal development, enhancing their overall performance and job satisfaction.

6. **Increased Team member Retention**: Profiling can help managers identify team member strengths and interests, allowing them to create development plans that align with team member goals. This can lead to increased job satisfaction and team member retention.

Overall, profiling your team can be an effective way to enhance communication, team performance, and individual development, leading to a more productive and satisfied team.

There are many profiling tools and some of the most popular are DiSC, Strength Finder, Myers-Briggs, Belbin.

Simple steps to get your A Team:

1. Ensure they agree with the **core values** of your business
2. Make sure they **understand what is required** in the role. This is where a letter of expectations is handy to go through with them (see letter of expectation). Ask them to feed back the role and ask how they would do it. This is to see they "get" what they need to do before they start the role. Unfortunately, you cannot be 100% sure until they are doing the role.
3. They must be **capable** of doing the role. The person must be able to carry out the role that they will be assigned to. This does not mean that they must already have done it but they are someone who will develop, learn and be capable of growing into the role.
   I have had many team members who have never done the role that I ask them to step up to and it would have been a steep learning curve for them. I was happy for them to take on the role as I knew they had the ability to learn, develop and ensure they do a great job. Yes, there will be mistakes on the way, which is all learning.

If they are not actually able to do what the role entails and never will be able to develop the skills to do the role then you do not want them, at least in that role. Again, you may not know if they ate capable of doing the role until, they start it.

4. They "**want" the role and to grow** to be good at the role. Attitude is a massive thing that I always look at in any team member. If they have the right attitude and are wanting to be part of the A team and ensure they learn and grow then this is a top one to have. Some people say that "you only need great attitude." This is not correct...... Great attitude without capability of doing the role and understanding of what is required will never work. You need the team member to have all three to be able to take up the A team spot. Not forgetting they must follow your core values (see core values).

***"The strength of the team is each individual member. The strength of each member is the team."***

Phil Jackson.

## Core Values

Having core values for any business is critical to make sure that everyone knows what behaviour is expected of them. It should be used when hiring to make sure all candidates for a role are aware of the core values and agree to them before they join. It should also be used in disciplinary situation and the person is told you have not met this core value.

If you do not have core values written up and publicly known, this does not mean you and your business do not have them, it just means that you have not articulated them.

You should then do a work shop to come up with your core values. Book in time with your team and write things on a board until you end up with a whole list of core values you like. Then bring it down to 3-7. The less the better and make sure they are easily remembered by all. You can create an acronym for the core values so you and your team remember them

For example.

Naylor Accountancy Services has 5 core values, iCARE:

**i**Ntegrity

**C**are

**A**ccountability

**R**espect

**E**xcellence

Intelligent Outsourcing has 7 core values, iCHARGE – as in charging a battery, being in charge and charging forward with growth.

**i**Ntegrity

**C**are

**H**ave fun

**A**ccountability

**R**espect

**G**rowth

**E**xcellence

Asda has 4 core values:

a. Service to our customers.

b. Respect for the individual.

c. Strive for excellence.

d. Act with integrity.

***"Your values become your destiny."***

Mahatma Gandhi

## Letter of expectation

A letter of expectations is basically what it says, a written down document stating exactly what you are expecting from someone in the position they hold addressed to them, hence a letter. It can be used in 2 different ways. One for an existing team member who is not fulfilling your expectations. Once your expectations are written down on paper it makes it perfectly clear to you and your team member what is required to meet your expectations. Once you have gone through it with the team member you give them the physical letter of expectation so they understand it. You should then finish off by ask them "do you agree with these expectations?." I would also say "if you go away and have any queries on it then let me know."

If you do not want to give the letter of expectation to the person as you fear they will take it personally and may leave and you do not want that. Then still write it for your own benefit but then instead of giving them the letter of expectations have conversations with them around what you are expecting and get their buy in and agreement. This is necessary for you to be clear of what you are expecting them to do in their role and also to ensure you do not make things worse for you and the practice as some people have egos that will not take the letter of expectation.

It can also be used when hiring a new team member. You create a letter expectations of what you will be expecting the new team member to do. This is different to job description as it is more in depth but will have elements of it in there. It is how you would expect the team member to behave, act and interact with people and more as well as the actual job required itself. We have used this when hiring someone new and then ensured the person agrees to our expectations.

Story of letter of Expectation.

The first time I had to use a letter of expectation was for someone who had just started with us and the team member sat next to them complained that she could not be in the office with them as they stank terribly of BO and were unkempt. The other team member stated they looked and smelt like a homeless person and this was a qualified senior accountant who was good at their job.

I had to do something quickly as there was an issue and the person would also be meeting with clients, so not a great ambassador for our accountancy practice despite being a great accountant. When interviewed and we met them for a follow-up get to know them lunch they had not exhibited any of this and were clean, smart and presentable.

I created a letter of expectation stating amongst other things:

"You are required to be smart and presentable for work which includes:

- haircut and trim beard at least every 6 weeks.
- Have a clean ironed shirt every day.
- Have clean clothes that do not carry an unpleasant odour in the office.
- Wearing clothes that fit properly.
- Always having clean hair.

- Ensure hair is clean cut and smart and representative of a professional person. I can share some examples of what I mean by this if required. "

I ended the letter stating

"I would like to support you with each of these points. If there is any matter that requires further clarification, please let me know by return and I will gladly assist. Any further breaches of the values or standards will result in disciplinary proceeding commencing. I trust this will not be necessary.

Yours Faithfully "

The person excepted the letter and made the changes required to meet the expectations. It was a matter of them being explained what was required as they were oblivious to the issue as that was just the way they had been for years.

## Team NOT Employees or staff

Do you currently use "staff" or "employee" when you talk about or with your accountancy team?

If so, I challenge you to make this simple change and use "Team," Team Member" and "Our Team" when talking to clients, your Team, friends and other accountants......basically anyone. You will keep using the old term but keep going and make sure you catch yourself when you use "staff" or "employee" about your team.

I have to admit you still need to use the HMRC and accountancy terms when required like "employee benefits", "employee NI", etc so you cannot do away with it totally.

So, always use the term Team, Team Member and Our Team (not "your" or "my" team if you can help it) as you could never do what you do without them, the Team. Then all know they are part of the same team and they are not your minion.

I have always done this in my UK accountancy practice and all the Team use it for each other too. I also use it in Intelligent Outsourcing and that I had to really train the team to use "team" and not employee or staff. Now it is natural.

Richard Branson uses term "teams" because he knows he can't do it by himself, that is the same for all of us.

## Recruitment and retention

Recruiting and retention of your Team is the hardest thing to do. There are loads of books written by gurus on recruitment and retention. Key for retention is you get the right people in the first time who buy into your vision and core values. You will always have team members leaving as you never know what is going on in their lives or heads. You must not beat yourself up about it and get straight onto recruiting a replacement.

- Know what you are looking for by creating the Avatar as already mentioned.
- Always ask for feedback from those that are leaving so you know what drove them to depart and if there are any changes you need to put in place. Be aware they may not be telling you the truth but there is always learning to be had from someone leaving.

Recruiting is currently a massive problem for accountancy practices with very few candidates and the salaries of good accountants has sky rocketed. From speaking to a lot of accountancy practice owners one thing they say is accountants in the UK can earn far more in commerce and industry and the work is less stressful so they are opting to move out of practice. This creates a big issue! Who will you get and how will the work get done?

I had the same issue when I was growing my accountancy practice. I wanted to ensure an excellent service and I was struggling to offer it as getting good accountants so close to London that I could afford (my practice is in Tunbridge Wells) and that wanted to work for a small accountancy practice was very difficult. That is what drove me to create an offshore team in the Philippines and create Intelligent Outsourcing with the help of local knowledge of Dee

Smith and Christine Sy. We then developed iO Academy to ensure all accountants were to a certain level and were continually developing to ensure an excellent service.

If you are struggling to get the team you want to do the compliance work you should consider creating a team offshore doing the compliance work for your accountancy practice. You would want them to use all your processes and systems so you are in control. At the same time, you want to partner with an offshore company that cares about making it work for you and has the UK accountancy knowledge and training support you will need (check out their core values). Then your UK team can focus on the client relationships and added value work.

See chapter on "Offshoring Team" if you want to know more.

**Create a Leadership team.**

Within your A-team you need people you can talk with on the same level about issues, strategy and vision. This is your leadership team. The leadership team may be small to start with as you do not have a big enough business or the right people to be on it, so ensure this grows as the business grows as you want to buy in from those doing the work and managing others. You want all the hats of the business to be covered by your leadership team and people can wear more than one hat, which will be the case at the start. As a business owner you wear all the hats at the start of your business unless you have a business partner. If you do not have anyone to be on the leadership team with you it is advisable to build a Mastermind Group with other friends who have accounting practices of their own or better still join an established Mastermind group like The Accountants Mastermind run by Simon Chaplin and Mark Swindle (I have been a member of this since 2016 and it has been invaluable for me).

When creating your leadership team, it is worth you knowing exactly what you are wanting from them and give them clarity of this. You want them to highlight issues as you will not know everything and the bigger you grow and/or get away from the doing of the compliance work and client interactions you will need to rely on issues being highlighted by the team.

You must have regular Leadership Team meetings, see the "Regular Meetings" section. This is key for them to feel empowered and you to feel secure that they have control of the business.

I have totally pulled away from all client relationships apart from some of my first clients who I have a strong relationship with and by having the leadership team with their clear responsibilities and regular meetings with KPIs that ensure things stay on track I can sleep easy at night. I know I have a great leadership team that can deal with the running of the business and issues. I am still in all the leadership meetings so I can guide and be part of discussions of issues after which we look at solutions and decide on the action(s) to take.

I have not abdicated responsibility of the business but delegated. I will step in and mentor and guide. Through regular meetings I know what is happening, what the issues are and help in discussing and creating solutions for the issues. Key is you cannot just turn your back on the business or you will lose it. There must be controls in place to ensure that everything functions as it should be and that you are aware of issues before they are too big....

I know of someone who had placed a Practice Manager in to look after his business and he did have what he thought was good data to manage the business but the service levels dropped and they lost over half the business. He learned a lot of lessons from that and mine to you is, be aware of what is happening in the business without doing all the work – delegate but never abdicate responsibility. After all, if anything happens it is you who takes ultimate responsibility and no one else!

***"Alone we can do so little; together we can do so much."***

Helen Keller

# Chapter 4

# RHYTHM OF THE BUSINESS

# 4. RHYTHM OF THE BUSINESS

It is critical that you bring a regular rhythm of how the business is run and communication happens and this comes through structuring it and sticking to it. You want your team to work as one and be able to be openly talk about an issues they see. Last thing you want is for a team member to feel that they have nothing to contribute and the issue they can see has just been totally neglected.

The rhythm of managing any business is all about what meetings you have and how you communicate in them. This encompasses the regularity, time they take, who is involved in them and what is discussed in them.

Below is how we operate in Naylor Accountancy Services and Intelligent Outsourcing and have created our "rhythm." It has been tried and tested and although sometimes it may seem too much, when missed out on the odd occasion that it has, you notice it and it impacts the rhythm...

I cannot explain how much this will help your accountancy practice if you follow a regular rhythm and as I see it as being so critical, I have highlighted exactly how we run them. To start with some team members thought it was too much but now they all see the importance of them and they hate to miss them when they are off.

I will start with the most frequent rhythm meeting and work up to the ones only done once a year.

**Daily Huddle**

This is where the team gets together every morning for 15 minutes tops and each person has 1-2 minutes to talk about what happened the previous day and what they are working on that day. If they need a hand or have any queries, they will mention them then too. This is the normal pulse for Naylor Accountancy Services as we have most of our accountants and two administrators in the Philippines with Intelligent Outsourcing so we need the team in the UK and Philippines to feel like they are part of the same team. The daily huddle is held on Teams video call and before that came into existence it was Skype.

Some people call it a "daily scrum" and is something that used to happen in the IT programme development team when I worked in the City of London, it was done standing in a circle on the open floor to ensure it was quick.
You can do regular weekly team huddles but I would not recommend anything longer. It really does help create the team atmosphere you want for any business.

## Weekly Leadership meetings

This is done on the same day and time each week and if people cannot make it then they just miss it and the meeting carries on. That is true if "you" are away, you just have someone else run the meeting. It is typically 1.5 hours long and starts on time and finishes on time.

In the meeting you would start with a few minutes with everyone just sharing anything interesting they have done or will be doing personally. This is just to get everyone engaged and help connect with each other.

Then go through your business data which is anything that you want to measure for your business that impacts if not moving in the direction required. For an accounting practice this could be:

1. Number of new clients signed up in the month
2. Number clients resigning
3. Number of accounts completed in the month so far
4. Number of Self-assessments completed in the month so far
5. Number of VAT returns done after a certain internal deadline. This could be the 25th of the month
6. Profit so far for the month
7. Turnover for the month
8. Debtors for the month
9. Whatever you want to measure

Then go through any actions that were created from the previous meeting. Every action created only has ONE person responsible for it which means that there is nowhere to hide... So, ask has it been done or not. Normally and action should be completed within the week but you can allow to move over for another week but anything more than 2 weeks may be an issue so you may need to discuss further.

Issues – finally establish the issues the business currently has and which is the most important one and then discuss the issue. The issue as it has been presented rarely is the real issue so make sure everyone is drilling down into it and probing to understand what all the issues are relating to the one described.
Once you have established what the real issue is then you should all brainstorm potential solutions. You will then be able to decide between your leadership team what the solution to the issue is you all want to do. The solution becomes an "action" and it is allocated to one of the leadership team to ensure it is carried out. They will report back on the action in the next weekly meeting.

Close the meeting on time. If you have not covered everything do not worry you can next week. If there is an urgent issue that needs to be resolved before the next meeting then book a separate meeting that week to cover it.

## 121 meetings

It is important to have regular one to one (121) meetings with your direct reports, this could be your entire team if you are not large or just the few in your leadership team. They would then have 121 meetings with their team, cascading down further if you are large.

In these 121 meetings you go through what they are working on led by them, what you see is important going forward, any issues they have and always ask them at the end of the meeting **"is there anything else?"** then pause, do not break the silence as some team members take a while to think, get the courage to say what is still on their mind.

Always ask this and train others to ask, "is there anything else?" at the end of the meeting.

You can do 121s weekly, bi weekly or monthly. I would not do less frequently than monthly and you can vary the frequency depending on what is going on in your business and how comfortable you are leaving the team members to get on with things without your guidance or knowledge of what is happening.

## Quarterly Review Meeting

Everyone has a 90-day attention span to focus on a project which is why the quarterly review meeting is critical and in it you will set the next quarterly projects and allocate each one to an individual to ensure there is one person responsible for it. This means it will get done. This meeting is a whole day. You may think that you will not have enough to talk about for a full day. We typically have ours starting 9am and finishing at 4pm with an hour for lunch and everyone is exhausted at the end! You can shorten it initially but you will soon want the full day. We did that initially and just overran. You do not want any distraction of incoming calls, emails and other team members. You can ensure this by having the meeting out of the office. We have our Naylor Accountancy Services quarterly review meeting in the board room of our shared offices and turn all emails off and ensure our out of office in emails are on and the rest of the team know not to disturb us unless urgent. We have 2 people dial in on Teams as they are based in the Philippines and are in the Intelligent Outsourcing board room.

Start the quarterly review meeting with positivity and have each person giving the following

a) what they think the biggest three achievements of the business in the last 90 days.
b) Their greatest personal accomplishment
c) What they are expecting of the day

Once this is complete you go through **the quarterly KPIs** you are measuring, the goals and the financials, only state if expectations were met or not. If they were not met then there could be an issue to discuss later in the meeting so have that written down to cover later in the meeting.

Then go through the **quarterly projects** that were set to get an update whether they are completed or not. If not completed then you need to decide on the following:

a) Carry forward
b) Reassign to another person
c) If virtually completed then move to the "to do."

## Review the Way Forward Plan

This is the vision, 10-year, 3 year and 1 year plan document created at the start of the year (see Way Forward Pan). It is key that everyone still believes in the this and if any changes are needed due to circumstances changing then this is the time to discuss this and agree any changes. It also ensures everyone is reminded of the Way Forward Plan to sharpen their focus on achieving what is expected.

Make sure you have a short 10–15-minute break after 2 hours as people will need a comfort break.

**Establish next Quarters Projects**

You may already have some quarterly projects to carry forward so add them to the list for the next quarter. Create a list of all that must get done in the next 90 days in order to you continue to meet your one-year plan and meet any new obligations.

Discuss which are the tops 3-8 projects that you all want to work on in the next quarter. Be careful to not overload the team with projects as then nothing will get done. It is better to have fewer so they can focus on them and complete them. You can then pick up the other projects in the preceding quarter.

Assign each quarterly project to a person. Again, this is to ensure it gets done as there is no one else responsible apart from that person. They can delegate and get others to work on the project too but it is their responsibility to ensure that the project is completed and no one else's.

The Quarterly Projects are created and must be documented with person responsible for it.

**Lunch** – ensure you know when you want to break for lunch and when you get to that time then finish off any discussion you are in the mid of and break. Then break for 45 minutes to an hour as you need to all eat.

Carry on where you broke off for lunch, you may have competed all the above already so just move on fitting within your own timeframe.

## Key Issues Discussed

Go through the list of issues you have for the business from the weekly meetings and that have been brought up from this quarterly meeting. If the new quarterly projects will be dealing with one of the issues, then remove it and then decide which are the top 3 issues.

Discuss the first top issue and establish if indeed the issue stated is the issue. Do dive down into the issue as it invariably is not the issue you need to deal with. Once you have talked over the issue, what it is, how it impacts the business and people, then look at potential solutions. Everyone should participate and give their views to get a good depth to the issue and potential solutions. Nothing is a bad idea; everything should be discussed.

Once all solutions have been brought forward then decide what solution you all agree the business should take. Add this solution to the "to-do list" and assign a person responsible for it.

Keep doing this moving onto the next issue until you run out of issues or you are 30 minutes near the end of the meeting. Then move into concluding of the quarterly review.

## Conclude

Confirm the projects for the next quarter and who is responsible and then do the same for projects or to-do's that have been created, are still live and who is responsible for them.

Ensure all are written down and circulated after the meeting. If the Way Forward Plan has changed then a new edited documented must be created and circulated to all.

Decide if a message needs to be given to the rest of the team on what you have decided in the meeting. If it does then ensure you communicate this and always best done in person in a companywide meeting or town hall. If all the team are present in the quarterly review meeting, then there is no need to consider this.

Ask all participants of the meeting if their expectations for the meeting were met. If not then ask for what specifically why and how they could ensure that their expectations are met next time.

## Annual Way Forward Planning Meeting

This is a critical meeting that you must have with your leadership team, if you are too small to have a leadership team you can just do this meeting by yourself. Reason for having the Annual Way Forward Planning Meeting is for you to create a plan that encompasses your vision, building it out and creating the steps you need to take in order to get to where you want. You want to do this with your leadership team so they all buy into it and have a say in creating it. This is so important as without others wanting to carry on the torch for the business as you cannot grow the business without this. If you are the only person creating it that is fine, if you have team you will want to share what you are happy sharing with them once you have created your Way Forward as this will help them understand what you are looking to achieve and why you are wanting to do what you have planned.

I did the Annual Way Forward Planning Meeting myself until I was in a position to create a leadership team for Naylor Accountancy Services. So, this is definitely something you should do whatever size you are.

Allow 2 days for the Annual Way Forward Planning Meeting and this should ideally be somewhere where you are not disturbed so out of the office is best as you do not want to be disturbed or distracted by the day-to-day operations of your accountancy practice.

I will break down the meeting so you can see the structure of this meeting which is simple.

*Day 1*

**Personal news** – start lightly with all participants mentioning something that that they have just done that was fun or of interest. This helps everyone to get to know each other better and ensures all have something to say at the start to get their talking juices started.

**Personal review of last year**

Each meeting participant needs to share the following:

- 3 biggest accomplishments of the business in the last year
- Personal accomplishments that mean the most in the last year
- Expectations for the Annual Way Forward Planning Meeting

**Review Previous Year**

This will already have been formulated by the person who responsible for the accountancy practice KPIs and financials and typically runs through the following:

- Achievements of the year (what was already mentioned by individuals should be in this plus others)
- Goals that have been achieved
- Financials – profits, debtors, cash, margin, etc.
- Non financials – number of clients, team members, etc.
- KPIs – where they met or not
- Projects last quarter – completed or not

Break a couple of hours after the start of the meeting with a 10–15-minute comfort break and then pick up again.

**SWOT analysis on the business**

I am sure you are familiar with a SWOT analysis as you must have done many but I will just highlight it and the reason for having to do one in your Annual Way Forward meeting.

SWOT analysis is a strategic planning tool used to evaluate the strengths, weaknesses, opportunities, and threats of a business or project. Here's a quick breakdown of each component:

**Strengths:** Internal factors that give an advantage, such as expertise, resources, or a strong brand.

**Weaknesses**: Internal factors that put the business at a disadvantage, such as poor management, lack of resources, or low team member morale.

**Opportunities**: External factors that can benefit the business, such as new market trends, emerging technologies, or changes in consumer behaviour.

**Threats**: External factors that can harm the business, such as increased competition, economic downturns, or regulatory changes.

SWOT analysis helps you make informed decisions and develop effective strategies by considering these four key elements.

By analysing each of these components, you can identify your competitive position and develop strategies to address areas of weakness and take advantage of opportunities. Add anything that comes up in the weakness to the issues list and potentially also some of the threats but only if you can do anything about them or make the issue have less impact.

Doing the SWOT analysis every year is a must as it ensures participation of everyone in the room, getting them to think about the business as a whole and helps getting them onboard with the creation of the Vision in the next steps.

Break for Lunch – do this whenever the time you decide to have lunch and then pick up where you left off afterwards. Allow up to 1 hour.

**10-year Vision**

Discuss or think about (if just you) what you want this to look like. For example, total turnover, profit margin, profit, how many clients, how many offices, how many team members, the average client fee. Put as much detail into this as possible.

This discussion is one of the most interesting if you have a leadership team and I have found that my 10-year vision has been stretched further by them as they can see as a team, we have a far bigger potential.

**Target market** – be clear what sort of clients you are focussing on. It does not mean you do not take on clients that do not fall into this category, it just gives you focus on who you're ideally looking to bring in.

**For example**:

i) Type of businesses you want – e.g., Tech companies; building companies; retail; dentists; doctors; agencies; creatives; trades....

ii) Turnover of the companies you would like - e.g., £100-£500k; £150k-£1m; £250-£2m, or whatever you are would like to target

iii) Number of business owners of the client you bring on – e.g., 1 business owner (this is the easiest as only one main decision maker)

iv) Number of team members they have

v) Location of the businesses

Confirm what your **Unique Selling Points** are and look to keep this to three. This should incorporate your culture, belief and what you do. For example, you can highlight one of your core values (see section on core values); how you operate through the use of technology; types of meetings; help companies grow......

Look at what you believe makes your accountancy practice unique when all three are together. This can be difficult to come up with so keep looking and as long as you have 3 USPs you can sell to clients you are there.

**Core values** – check all is still in agreement with the core values. If not then debate this as all must agree the core values and it may need some tweaking of there is reason to make a change. If this is the case their will be an educational communication needed to the rest of the team explaining the change and why.

You need to keep discussing and debating until you and your leadership team are all in agreement with the 10-year vision. This will inspire the leadership team as they will be totally bought into the vision as they helped create it. This is dynamite and will mean full engagement in the process in getting the business there. This is exactly what I have experienced with my leadership in Naylor Accountancy Services and my other business Intelligent Outsourcing. In fact, they made the vision grandeur that I had initially created myself.

**3-year Picture**

Once you have agreed your 10-year vision you move onto the 3-year picture. Create this picture together so they can really smell and feel what it looks like. Get a clear picture with the date stated and then points on what it will look like by that date.

For example:

Future date – 3 years on.

<u>Measurables</u>

- Revenue
- Profit
- Margin
- Number of clients
- Average fee per client

<u>What it looks like</u>

- Number of offices & locations
- Number of team members
- Number Client managers
- Number of acquisitions
- Role you will have then
- Leadership team in place that is strong
- Number of potential client enquiries per month
- Part of a mastermind group
- What technology you will have in place
- Regular leadership meetings – Weekly, quarterly and annual
- All clients do an Annual Plan with us
- Offshoring team doing all the compliance work

Make sure all the leadership team still agree with your businesses core values (see section on core values). If not then discuss and agree on what they should be. Add the core values to your vision as everyone must believe and abide by the core values.

**1-year plan**

First, I would write a list of the issues that your accountancy practice has. This will help you create the one-year plan as some of the goals will be there as a solution to an issue

With the 3-year picture created you can then easily see what you need to do the next 12 months. Again, this would have the measurables you want to achieve at the end of the year and the goals within he business you want to achieve over the 12 months.

For example:

Future date 1 year on.

Measurables

- Revenue
- Profit
- Margin
- Number of clients
- Average fee per client

Goals for the year

- Credit control process in place

- Happiness survey to send to clients and team members create and send out with process in place
- KPIs implemented for every team member and a monthly meeting with team to go through them
- Fee reviews all clients
- Acquisition
- Hire new Client manager
- Create an offshore team to do bookkeeping, VAT, payroll and yearend accounts

**End day 1** – you should end the day once you have been at it for 6 hours as you will be shattered, but definitely do not go over 7 hours. We tend to do 9am to 4pm with breaks as mentioned.

## DAY 2

Pick up the second day where you left of the first day. You may have gone slower or quicker, key is to just follow an agenda and keep to it so you get everything done. You may need to discuss some areas for longer than others which is fine if you get everyone on the same page.

**Establish the next quarters projects**

Create a list of all that must get done in the next 90 days to you continue to meet your one-year plan.

Discuss which are the tops 3-8 projects that you want to work on in the next quarter. Do not overload with projects as then nothing will get done. It is better to have fewer so the team can focus on them and complete them. You can then pick up the other projects in the preceding quarter.

Assign each quarterly project to a person. Again, this is to ensure it gets done as there is no one else responsible apart from that person. They can delegate and get others to work on the project too, but it is their responsibility to ensure that the project is completed and no one else's.

The Quarterly Projects are created and must be documented with person responsible for it.

Break a couple of hours after starting the meeting with a 10–15-minute comfort break and then pick up again.

Break for Lunch – do this whenever the time you decide to have lunch and then pick up where you left off afterwards. Allow up to 1 hour.

**Key Issues Discussed**

Go through the list of issues you have including those that you have added during this Annual Way Forward meeting. If the new quarterly projects will be dealing with one of the issues, then remove it and then decide which are the top 3 issues.

Discuss the first top issue and establish if indeed the issue stated is the issue. Do dive down into the issue as it invariably is not the issue you need to deal with. Once you have talked over the issue, what it is, how it impacts the business and people, then look at potential solutions. Everyone should participate and give their views to get a good depth to the issue and potential solutions. Nothing is a bad idea; everything should be discussed.

Once all solutions have been discussed you must collectively decide what solution the business should take. Add this solution to the "to-do list" and assign a person responsible for it.

Keep doing this moving onto the next issue until you run out of issues or you are 1 hour near the end of the meeting. Then move into concluding of the meeting.

**Conclude**

Confirm the projects for the next quarter and who is responsible and then do the same for to-do's that created and are still active ensuring person responsible is aware of them.

Ensure all are written down and circulated after the meeting.

Talk through the Way Forward you have just created highlighting the 10-year vision, 3-year view and 1 year plan. You want everyone to visualise what the accountancy practice will look like in if you all follow the steps you have laid out.

Decide what message needs to be given to the rest of the team about the Way Forward you have just created or updated. Ensure you communicate this and it is always best done in person in a companywide meeting or town hall or personally by the leadership team to their direct reports.

If all the team are present in Annual Way Forward Planning meeting, then there is no need to consider this.

Ask all participants of the meeting for feedback on the meeting and if their expectations for the meeting were met. If not then ask why and how you could ensure that their expectations are met next time.

You always want to ask how a meeting went and if it did not go well then you want to know how to make the meetings better next time so always ask for feedback.

## Rules of a meeting

I have done so many meetings and one thing I hate is when I have a meeting and no one is engaged in it apart from me……have you have had that. There is no point having a meeting if others are not participating and sharing their thoughts and experiences, you may as well say here you are you have to do this, now go away and do it.

The reason for creating a team is that you want them to be able to think independently so they can act without you having to constantly tell them what to do next. You especially want them to tell you when something is not going well so you can all discuss what should be done. If the team member just carries on because you have told them to do it although they know it is wrong or a waste of time but they do not feel like they can say anything to you because you are the boss, then everyone is wasting time and can end up costing you money. Better for team members to realise they can challenge and must always be engaged. If they challenge a decision, you have made yet you still think it is the correct way forward, they must carry on with the task, the difference is you have heard their reasoning and then you can explain your reasoning to carry on. They will feel listened to as long as you explain why you are not taking the route they suggest.

When I start a team meeting especially the weekly meeting, quarterly review meeting and the annual way forward meeting I start it with the following reminder of what I am expecting from them in the meeting with the acronym **PHOOD** with a silent "f" for "ph" so it is **"FOOD" for thought before you start the meeting.**

- **Participation** - all must be 100% taking part in the meeting with discussions and no work emails as all must be focussed on the meeting as we want to hear all perspectives
- **Have fun** – one thing we look to do is have fun at work, which does not mean that the team are having fun all the time and not focusing on work. It means we want them to enjoy being at work and are happy being at work, we spend most of our week at work.
- **Optimism** – do not take a doom and gloom scenario as the default but that all can be done with a plan in place and steps to execute it.
- **Ownership** – take ownership of your actions and what you are responsible for and do not blame others and make excuses.
- **Do not think you know everything** – it is key you "listen" to others and be open to hear what others say so do not make your mind up before you hear other points of view.

# Chapter 5

# BUSINESS STRUCTURE

# 5. BUSINESS STRUCTURE

## Create systems and procedures

I think it is important to define what a system is as this highlights its importance.  A business system is a defined set of principles, practices and procedures that are applied to specific activities to achieve a specific result.

Having an accountancy practice so much of what is done is the same thing being done repeatedly so you want to ensure that everyone is doing the jobs consistently to the standard you want. The only way you can ensure this is to create systems and procedures that the team must follow when they do a job like a VAT return, yearend accounts, self-assessment or onboarding a new client. These systems and procedures must be written up and then improved whenever required ensuring everyone is aware of any improvement to the procedures. Everyone in the team who needs to do the procedure must have access to the write up. There is process management software you can use to write up all procedures like SweetProcess but Microsoft Word works well.

Systems and procedures are critical components of any business let alone an accountancy practice as they provide structure, consistency, and clarity in operations. By defining and documenting procedures, a business can ensure that all team members understand their roles and responsibilities, as well as how to perform their tasks effectively and efficiently.

One of the primary benefits of having well-defined systems and procedures is that it can help to create a consistent level of service quality. By following a set of established steps, team members can deliver the same level of quality regardless of who is performing the task. This consistency is essential for building a reputation for excellent service, which can lead to increased client/customer satisfaction and loyalty.

Another advantage of having systems and procedures in place is that they can help to minimise errors, mistakes, and accidents. By outlining the steps needed to perform a task correctly, potential problems can be identified and addressed before they occur. Additionally, by documenting the steps, team members can refer back to the procedures if they are unsure of how to perform a task, reducing the likelihood of errors or mistakes.

Having written procedures in place ensures that all team members are on the same page and have a clear understanding of what is expected of them. This can help to prevent misunderstandings or confusion, particularly in situations where multiple team members are involved in completing a task. It also stops everyone doing their job differently and missing out on steps.

Finally, it is essential to update systems and procedures when issues or mistakes occur. This allows you and the team to learn from mistakes and prevent them from happening again in the future. By continuously improving processes and procedures, you can become more efficient, effective, and successful. We have our ongoing "project perfect" in Naylor Accountancy Services and whenever a mistake happens, we add it to out project perfect list and we discuss the issue in our weekly meeting to come up with a solution as to what we can do to mitigate it happening again. We then add this to our procedures for the job and let all the team know of the change.

There are many different systems that you should have procedures written up for and you can use technology to help with many of these to ensure constancy, speed and ability to delegate. Here are a few examples of systems for accountancy practices:

- Onboarding a new client system
- Pricing system – GoProposal software can help with this and other pricing systems.
- Sales system - I recommend you read or listen to "Selling To Serve: The Breakthrough Sales System For Accountants" by James Ashford as this gives you loads of good ideas on this.
- Debtors' system
- Billing system
- Workflow system
- KPI system - I recommend you read or listen to "Banish the Bottleneck: 7 savvy steps to grow the (almost) perfect team for your accountancy practice" by Simon Chaplin as this gives loads of ideas.
- Client/customer service system
- Yearend accounts system
- VAT production system
- Self-assessment system
- Management accounts system
- Payroll and CIS system

Each one of the systems above could have a book written about them on their own and I have highlighted two further books that go into great detail on the respective system above. To me both these books are a must read for accountancy practice owners.

You may be concerned that you personally need to write up all the procedures but that is not the case. You should get your team to write them up and then you can review them. Key is to have something written up that can then be improved on as is required. When we are training someone new up on a procedure they will go through it, update it and improve it if required.

Ideally you want to have the systems run the business and the team run the systems. What this means is that anyone can take over the job if someone leaves and you can retain the desired level of service.

***"Great systems and procedures are the backbone of any successful business."***

Peter Drucker

## Organisational Structure and functions

Any business must have an organisational structure with functions being carried out by various team members and there is no difference for accounting practices.

As a business owner who has their own accountancy practice you must initially are in charge and more than likely carry out all the functions of your organisation without even thinking about it. It is worth being aware of the different functions so that you can look to pass on the responsibilities for the function as you grow and have team members who are able to take it on or you are able to outsource it although ultimate responsibility must lie within your business.

There are effectively 10 different functions or departments that any business has and you may take most of these on yet you need to delegate responsibility for the various functions where possible (see Chapter on Delegation).

The 10 functions of your business are:

1. Shareholder
2. Director/Visionary
3. Primary Leader
4. Service/Product Development
5. Operations
6. Marketing
7. Sales
8. Finance
9. HR
10. Admin/IT

You can only have one primary leader of the business and only one person can be responsible for a function but one person can have more than one function under them. Having a function responsibility does not mean that you have to do the work as you will no doubt have people to delegate to, but you are ultimately responsible for the tasks under that function and you must ensure that projects and tasks under that function are carried out and not blame anyone but yourself if not.

Structure of 10 functions in relation to each other:

The strategic nature of the business are the Shareholders and directors who create the vision and direction of your business. You are definitely sitting with these functions and you should have your leadership team involved in creating the vision that sets the direction. See Annual Way Forward Meeting in the chapter on "Rhythm of the Business."

The rest of the functions are operational with the Primary Leader being the one leader of the business in charge of making the vision happen, this is typically a CEO or General Manager in a large organisation and more than likely you. This is the function that you ultimately want to delegate to someone else if you want to be able to have others run your accountancy practice and you focus on the strategy and ways of spending your time how you want to. However, this is not something we all want to achieve and you may enjoy being the Primary Leaders as well as doing the strategic work. As mentioned, one can have more than one function and typically a business owner will have all the functions at the start of the business.

Each function has different responsibilities and although the names are self-explanatory you should ensure the roles of each are specified and this is why each task or project created is allocated to one person and this should be the person under that function. See the chapter on Rhythm of the Business as this describes how this works in practice.

Key responsibilities of each function must be clear and written down along with tasks. Take a look at the chapter on Team as this talks into ensuring there is a clear job description with expectations, priorities, etc.

By writing out the key responsibilities of each function you ensure that no area is neglected and if they are all with you then if you are able to you should delegate what you can. Do empower others to take on the responsibilities of that function and be careful not to take it over yourself as you will have been used to doing it yourself. Mentor the person and allow them to make mistakes as long as they keep moving forward.

Create an organisation chart with the people responsible for each function so this is visible to all even if you are taking on all or most of the functions. This brings clarity to others and you.

***"Organisations which design systems that are effective are those that are able to attract and retain the best employees."***

W. Edwards Deming

## Agendas

Agendas are important for meetings because they provide a structure and a roadmap for the discussion that will take place. Without an agenda, meetings can quickly become disorganised, unfocused, and unproductive. I have done too many without an agenda thinking I have it all in my head only to forget to go through one of the things I wanted to. Worse is someone calls a meeting with me and they have no agenda on what they want to talk through and we waste time talking about things that are not important.

Here are some specific reasons why agendas are important for meetings:

1. **Help participants prepare**: An agenda allows attendees to prepare for the meeting by knowing the topics to be discussed, the goals to be achieved, and any information they need to bring with them.
2. **Keep meetings on track**: An agenda sets the framework for the meeting and helps keep discussions focused on the topics at hand. This can prevent the meeting from going off-topic, getting side-tracked, or going over time.
3. **Ensure that important topics are addressed**: By outlining the key points to be discussed, an agenda ensures that important topics are not overlooked or forgotten.
4. **Facilitate participation**: When attendees know what will be discussed, they are more likely to participate actively and contribute meaningfully to the meeting.
5. **Provide a record of the meeting**: Agendas can be used to document what was discussed, decisions made, and action items assigned, which can be used as a reference for future meetings or to track progress on action items.

You will see the chapter “Rhythm of the Business” that there is a structure to them with an agenda. The one that is more off-piste is the 121 meeting as although a basic agenda it is not specific and can be just a chat to see how everything is going for the team member.

Overall, agendas are important for meetings because they help ensure that the meeting is productive, efficient, and achieves its objectives.

***"An agenda clarifies the purpose of the meeting and what you want to accomplish."***

Harvey Mackay

# Chapter 6

# OFFSHORING TEAM and OUTSOURCING

# 6. OFFSHORING TEAM and OUTSOURCING

I will start by defining "offshoring" as it can be confusing. Offshoring is a subset of outsourcing so it is easy to get mixed up, as for an accountancy practice you have two choices if you are looking to bring in external help to get your compliance work done. You can either:

1. **Outsource the work** to a third party using their systems and procedures, you have to give them the work in a certain format and then you receive it back to review. The person will more than likely be different each time so they will not know the clients or know how you want things.
2. **Offshore the work with a team exclusively** working for you using your systems and processes that you in control of. They will get to know your clients and learn how you want things done. They must be integrated into your existing team so they feel part of your team.

Creating your offshore team, in my opinion, is far more effective so it is an "intelligent" way to outsource work for any accountancy practice. Offshoring is where you have someone who works for you in another country that is more cost effective and where the supply of accountants is better than the home country.

You can get a FREE Whitepaper of an in-depth independent analysis on offshoring for accountants if you go to the intelligentoutsourcing.co.uk website.

An Offshore Team is one which uses all your accountancy practices systems and processes and the Team only work for your practice as part of your accountancy team. They should be totally integrated with your existing accountancy practice team.

One way that you can create the space and time to be able to focus on added value work, growing your business and on doing the things you want to do is by creating an offshore team. This is what I did with Naylor Accountancy Services. I was struggling to get local accountants to join the practice and at the start I did not have enough profit to warrant paying for a fully qualified accountant with experience. Creating an offshore team meant that I could get all the compliance and bookkeeping done by others who were also able to source the data and information directly with the clients which saved me further time as I did not need to email clients asking questions or requesting or chasing for information or documents. Emails take up so much time as I am sure they do for you too.

Key is that your offshore team learn from mistakes that are made as they are the same people doing your work just as if there was someone in the UK working directly for you doing the work.

I started with my offshore team just doing bookkeeping and then moved to VAT, payroll and then yearend accounts. Finally, we got them to do self-assessments too and management accounts. All the way through the offshore team used and are still using my Naylor Accountancy Services systems and processes. They help improve these processes and systems and come up with solutions and improvements as well as well as writing the procedures.

As well as my accountancy practice I have **Intelligent Outsourcing Ltd** and we find that most of our accountancy practice partners start with bookkeeping and VAT on their first offshore team member(s) and then grow the team and capacity to take on payroll, yearend accounts and management accounts.

We do have one very prominent and successful accountancy practice who started their offshore accounting team with Intelligent Outsourcing with the high value work with them doing management reporting and analysis and yearend accounts only. They created an Offshore Team of experienced accountants with Intelligent Outsourcing. They now have 7 offshore team members with us and are always recommended to others to work with Intelligent Outsourcing.

We have another large prominent accountancy practice who only started July 2022 and they had 5 offshore team members with Intelligent Outsourcing within 5 months and are still growing their offshore team.

We do also have small practices who just need one person to take on compliance and bookkeeping tasks from them so that they can focus on growing the practice. If they carried on doing the compliance work then they would never grow as they are just focussing on the doing of the work. This gives them a team member who they can rely on and that is able to communicate directly with the client so it is not all funnelling through them, if they want that and save themselves time and increasing the service to the client as the offshore team member will respond to the email quicker.

Requesting or chasing for information or documents takes up so much time for all accountants and is what holds up compliance work. So, having an offshore team that can focus on doing this as part of their job saves your UK team time to focus on the client added value, meetings, tax planning, new client generation, upselling or whatever else you want them to do which is higher value.

For Naylor Accountancy Services I have my Offshore team connect and talk directly to clients and we have done special vocal coaching with the admin team members who answer the phone for the practice.

Once you have started to create an offshore team, I would always suggest contemplating getting an admin person when the time is right for you. This helps with requesting and chasing for information and documents rather than the accountants always having to do this, that way they can concentrate on the compliance work themselves. There are loads of tasks that an admin can do for your practice and here are some examples:

Admin work:

- Email clients requesting yearend accounts documents.
- Email clients requesting self-assessment documents.
- Email clients requesting documents required to set up a Ltd company.
- Email clients chasing for information already requested until receive it.
- Call clients to ask for when to expect information or documents when email chasing has been ignored.
- Set up Ltd Companies and send information to clients once done.
- Onboard clients sending out emails requesting information and documents.
- Set up all Jobs for new work orders or new clients on the practice management system.
- Update all KPI data required.
- Check all work has been invoiced.

- Review client fees and bring up with relevant person if fee needs to change.
- Ad hoc work
- Company Secretariate work – change address with HMRC and Companies House, new directors add along with all documentation signed by clients, new shareholding set up and create documents for signing and file; change in directors; change in company name; etc…..
- Answer phones

Benefits of creating an offshore team:

1. Talented accountants
2. Cost effective
3. Someone else deals with the HR
4. Use your systems and processes
5. Can do the work you want them to do

Key to making offshoring work:

1. Make the offshore team feel part of your whole accountancy practice
2. Make sure all your existing team are happy about you having offshored team members
3. Regular team meeting with all – daily huddles or weekly or monthly at the very least
4. Have them in an office not WFH

There is loads more that can be said on offshoring and how to make is a success. If you want to find out more you can come to one of my regular webinars or go to the intelligentoutsourcing.co.uk website and there are loads of material on I am including videos, testimonials and as mentioned early a free Whitepaper on

Go to our website on intelligentoutsourcing.co.uk if you want to hear what others say about offshoring and how we make it work with iO Academy at the heart of it.

# Summary

# Summary

You should be aware of what will ensure that you have an ineffective accountancy practice and then look at what you need to do to "get the accounting practice you want", giving you the freedom that you want to be that time, financial or mind freedom.

There are 6 main things you must focus on.

The first is **"You"** as without you understanding "You" then it will be an uphill battle. Make sure "you" know what you want and then that you act in a way that will give you the business you want.

**"Team"** is the thing you must get right as without your A-Team you will have no chance to get the accounting practice you want.

The **"rhythm of the business"** is simple to do but is something that you must get in place and then follow religiously whatever you decide your rhythm is. Even if sometimes you think it is overkill do not stop it.

"**Services"** are the business of any accountancy practice and the compliance element of this should happen smoothly without much intervention so you can focus on the client relationship and added value work.

**"Business structure"** is a must to understand and ensure all your team have clarity on. Get the systems and procedures all written up and constantly improved on.

The final thing that could make a massive difference to allowing you to get the accountancy practice you want is creating an **"offshore team."**

Offshoring can play a major role in ensuring you get the accounting practice you want just as it has for me with Naylor Accountancy Services and other Intelligent Outsourcing clients.

All the best in creating the accountancy practice you want and if you have already got it then do not sit on your laurels and ensure you keep improving.

# Appendix

## a) Why #hamster?

You may have noticed my headline on LinkedIn is "Let us be your **Hamster** and save you time to grow your business or allow you to breathe" and that I use **#hamster** for sign off on LinkedIn. You will no doubt think it is odd......you may think this Nikolai Naylor is an accountant with an accountancy practice and an outsourcing offshore business, why on earth would he use #hamster and have such a weird headline.

So let me tell you the story behind #hamster.

I talk to a lot of accountants and the two things most complain about are:

1. Working too many hours and running around like a "hamster" in a wheel to get all the work done and talk to clients.
2. Not able to find any accountants to take on the compliance work.

I have actually had several accountants say, "I am running around like a **hamster** in a wheel." I started to reply to them, "let us, Intelligent Outsourcing, be your **hamster** and do all your compliance work, then you can focus on the clients and the added value."

That led to me creating the LinkedIn headline of "Let us be your hamster and save you time to grow your business or allow you to breathe" as this resonated with the pain that we can help alleviate for accountants.

Then the simple **#hamster** sign off on posts was created. You will see the rest of Intelligent Outsourcing using **#hamster** now as well.

I hope you can now see the logic to the use have "#hamster."

The great thing is that everyone can easily remember **#hamster** as it is short and odd for an outsourcing offshore business. I have even been called the hamster guy by someone......not sure that is a good thing or not .......

## b) Selling your practice?

If you are considering selling your practice it is worth doing all you can so that it is not an issue if you step back so that you do not lose on the clawback when clients leave the practice you sell to within the first 2 years of the sale.

With Naylor Accountancy Services we have done one acquisition already and looking to complete the next one in the summer of 2023. We will then be looking to do an acquisition per year as with Intelligent Outsourcing their supporting Naylor Accountancy Services we know we can deliver a great service and take on new clients en mass and integrate them all. If you are looking to sell your practice, please do reach out to me, Nikolai Naylor, on LinkedIn as we will be getting our acquisition pipeline ready for the next 10 years. Even if you are not thinking about selling now but are within 10 years it is worth reaching out as we are planning ahead.

It is worth noting that if you do have an offshore team with Intelligent Outsourcing and you want to sell your accounting practice it will be favourable to us and we would want to place you ahead of any other acquisition in the pipeline.

# Acknowledgments

It is amazing when you think of whom you would like to thank. There are always so many people that help you along your journey and we are always learning. I would like to just thank everyone I know and have met over my many years on this Earth as every one of you has had an impact in some way.

I have to start by thanking the one person who pushed me to write this book and ensure I stayed on track, so a massive thank you to Ashley Leeds. His positivity, energy, and great creativity are something I have not come across in another person before and I feel blessed that our paths have crossed.

My family has been immense support throughout running my businesses, with my lovely wife Kate putting up with my long hours at the start and having to sort the kids out when I am in the Philippines visiting the Intelligent Outsourcing team out there whilst still having her own stellar career. My daughter Grace inspired me to realise that I can write a book as she has already written 3 books and she's only 17. My son Christian for always smiling and being a fellow fact nerd and someone I can throw a rugby ball around with.

There would be no Intelligent Outsourcing without Dee Smith and Christine Sy, so a massive thank you to both of them.

David Parker inspired me to set up my own accountancy practice Naylor Accountancy Services and helped me at the start, so a huge thanks.

Naylor Accountancy Services team and Intelligent Outsourcing team present and past a big thank you for all their dedication and for helping on the journey.

The leadership team of Intelligent Outsourcing and Naylor Accountancy Services without whom I would not be able to "let go" and neither business would be growing. So, thanks to Dee Smith, Christine Sy, Korina Cue, Jetaime Villamar, Glenny Pili, Pauline Sebastian, Michael Lewis, Franz Sebastian, and Andy Jordan.

Simon Chaplin a giant thanks for challenging me from the very start when I joined his mastermind group. That was pivotal for helping me change my mindset and it made me realise that running your accountancy practice was not just about knowing what you need to do tax and compliance-wise. He opened up my eyes to new ideas, and to books through the speakers we had and from recommendations from other mastermind members. I was inspired to learn more, change things, and continually self-develop.

My Mastermind group current and past have always been open and allowed me to continue to learn from them and I really appreciate their support. Thanks to Philip Knight, Jeremy Buitenhuis, Kim Marlor, Chris Bond, Michael Hemme, Nathan Hopkins, Wijay Kanagasundaram, David Gormer, Paul Meades, Jane Capel, Jo Whitehead, Stuart Ramsay, and of course Mark Swindale.

Mark Allen for his stories, advice, and for creating TAG of which we are founding members. I met Mark at my first accountancy conference and he has been inspirational on his journey, especially in the way he handled and came out of his life-threatening predicament. We also love Tae Kwon Do.

Paul Barnes and James Ashford I want to thank for being the first to invite me to speak publicly about our Intelligent Outsourcing proposition on the GoProposal webinar back in August 2019 "How, When & Why Should My Accountancy Firm Offshore?" The video has had 639 views which to me, is a lot.

Filipino people who are so friendly and smiley and always want to please. I think of them when things are tough and think of our outreach that touches those that have so little.

Daniel Priestly —

Printed in Great Britain
by Amazon

21628761R00071